DĀNA

The Practice of Giving

Selected Essays

Edited by Bhikkhu Bodhi

BUDDHIST PUBLICATION SOCIETY
KANDY SRI LANKA

Published in 1990

Buddhist Publication Society
P.O. Box 61
54, Sangharaja Mawatha
Kandy, Sri Lanka

ISBN 955-24-0077-5

Typeset at the BPS using an Atari 1040ST
computer and Signum 2.0 software.
Text set in Antique Roman.

Offset in Sri Lanka by
Karunaratne & Sons Ltd.
647, Kularatne Mawatha
Colombo 10

THE WHEEL PUBLICATION NO. 367/369

CONTENTS

INTRODUCTION

Bhikkhu Bodhi

The practice of giving is universally recognized as one of the most basic human virtues, a quality that testifies to the depth of one's humanity and one's capacity for self-transcendence. In the teaching of the Buddha, too, the practice of giving claims a place of special eminence, one which singles it out as being in a sense the foundation and seed of spiritual development. In the Pali suttas we read time and again that "talk on giving" (*dānakathā*) was invariably the first topic to be discussed by the Buddha in his "graduated exposition" of the Dhamma. Whenever the Buddha delivered a discourse to an audience of people who had not yet come to regard him as their teacher, he would start by emphasizing the value of giving. Only after his audience had come to appreciate this virtue would he introduce other aspects of his teaching, such as morality, the law of kamma, and the benefits in renunciation, and only after all these principles had made their impact on the minds of his listeners would he expound to them that unique discovery of the Awakened Ones, the Four Noble Truths.

Strictly speaking, giving does not appear in its own right among the factors of the Noble Eightfold Path, nor does it enter among the other requisites of enlightenment (*bodhipakkhiyā dhammā*). Most probably it has been excluded from these groupings because the practice of giving does not by its own nature conduce directly and immediately to the arising of insight and the realization of the Four Noble Truths. Giving functions in the Buddhist discipline in a different capacity. It does not come at the apex of the path, as a factor constituent of the process of awakening, but rather it serves as a basis and preparation which underlies and quietly supports the entire endeavour to free the mind from the defilements.

Nevertheless, though giving is not counted directly among the factors of the path, its contribution to progress along the road to liberation should not be overlooked or underestimated. The prominence of this contribution is underscored by the place which the Buddha assigns to giving in various sets of practices he has laid down for his followers. Besides appearing as the first topic in the graduated exposition of the Dhamma, the practice of giving also figures as the first of the three bases of meritorious deeds (*puññakiriyavatthu*), as the first of the four means of benefitting others (*sangahavatthu*), and as the first of the ten *pāramis* or "perfections." The latter are the sublime virtues to be cultivated by all aspirants to enlightenment, and to the most exalted degree by those who follow the way of the Bodhisatta aimed at the supreme enlightenment of perfect Buddhahood.

Regarded from another angle, giving can also be identified with the personal quality of generosity (*cāga*). This angle highlights the practice of giving, not as the outwardly manifest act by which an object is transferred from oneself to others, but as the inward disposition to give, a disposition which is strengthened by outward acts of giving and which in turn makes possible still more demanding acts of self-sacrifice. Generosity is included among the essential attributes of the *sappurisa*, the good or superior person, along with such other qualities as faith, morality, learning and wisdom. Viewed as the quality of generosity, giving has a particularly intimate connection to the entire movement of the Buddha's path. For the goal of the path is the destruction of greed, hate and delusion, and the cultivation of generosity directly debilitates greed and hate, while facilitating that pliancy of mind that allows for the eradication of delusion.

The present *Wheel* publication has been compiled in order to explore in greater depth this cardinal Buddhist virtue, the practice of giving, which in writings on applied Buddhism is so often taken for granted that it is usually passed over without comment. In this issue four practising Buddhists of today, all of whom combine a textual knowledge of the Buddha's teachings with a personal commitment to the path, set forth their understanding of the various aspects of giving and examine it in relation to the wider body of Dhamma practice.

The collection concludes with a translation of an older document—the description of the Bodhisatta's practice of giving by the medieval commentator, Ācariya Dhammapāla. This has been extracted from his Treatise on the Pāramis, found in his commentary to the Cariyāpiṭaka.

THE PRACTICE OF GIVING

Susan Elbaum Jootla

Giving (*dāna*) is one of the essential preliminary steps of Buddhist practice. When practised in itself, it is a basis of merit or wholesome kamma. When coupled with morality, concentration and insight, it leads ultimately to liberation from *saṁsāra*, the cycle of repeated existence. Even those who are well-established on the path to emancipation continue to practise giving as it is conducive to wealth, beauty and pleasure in their remaining lifetimes. Bodhisattas complete the *dānapārami* or perfection of giving to the ultimate degree by happily donating their limbs and their very lives to help other beings.

Like all good deeds, an act of giving will bring us happiness in the future, in accordance with the kammic law of cause and effect taught by the Buddha. Giving yields benefits in the present life and in lives to come whether or not we are aware of this fact, but

---

The inspiration and basic material for this essay come from *The Perfection of Generosity (Dāna Pārami)*, by Saya U Chit Tin, published as No. 3 in the Dhamma Series of the Sayagyi U Ba Khin Memorial Trust, U.K., Splatts House, Heddington near Calne, Wiltshire, England. I am deeply grateful to Saya U Chit Tin and to all the other teachers associated with the International Meditation Centres at Heddington, U.K. and Rangoon, Burma.

when the volition is accompanied by understanding, we can greatly increase the merits earned by our gifts.

The amount of merit gained varies according to three factors: the quality of the donor's motive, the spiritual purity of the recipient, and the kind and size of the gift. Since we have to experience the results of our actions, and good deeds lead to good results and bad deeds to bad results, it is sensible to try to create as much good kamma as possible. In the practice of giving, this would mean keeping one's mind pure in the act of giving, selecting the worthiest recipients available, and choosing the most appropriate and generous gifts one can afford.

The Factor of Volition

The volition of the donor before, during and after the act of generosity is the most important of the three factors involved in the practice of giving: "If we have no control over our minds we will not choose proper gifts, the best recipient . . . , we will be unable to prepare them properly. And we may be foolish enough to regret having made them afterwards."[1] Buddhist teaching devotes special attention to the psychological basis of giving, distinguishing among the different states of mind with which one may give. A fundamental distinction is made between acts of giving that lack wisdom and those that are accompanied by wisdom, the latter being superior to the former. An example of a very elementary kind of giving would be

1. U Chit Tin, *The Perfection of Generosity*, Introduction.

the case of a young girl who places a flower on the household shrine simply because her mother tells her to do so, without having any idea of the significance of her act.

Generosity associated with wisdom before, during and after the act is the highest type of giving. Three examples of wise giving are: giving with the clear understanding that according to the kammic law of cause and effect, the generous act will bring beneficial results in the future; giving while aware that the gift, the recipient and the giver are all impermanent; and giving with the aim of enhancing one's efforts to become enlightened. As the giving of a gift takes a certain amount of time, a single act of giving may be accompanied by each of these three types of understanding at a different stage in the process.

The most excellent motive for giving is the intention that it strengthen one's efforts to attain Nibbāna. Liberation is achieved by eliminating all the mental defilements (*kilesa*), which are rooted in the delusion of a controlling and lasting "I." Once this illusion is eradicated, selfish thoughts can no longer arise. If we aspire to ultimate peace and purity by practising generosity, we will be developing the *dāna pārami*, the perfection of giving, building up a store of merit that will bear its full fruit with our attainment of enlightenment. As we progress towards that goal, the volition involved in acts of giving will assist us by contributing towards the pliancy of the mind, an essential asset in developing concentration and wisdom, the prime requisites of liberation.

Ariyas—noble ones, those who have attained any

of the four stages of holiness—always give with pure volition because their minds function on the basis of wisdom. Those below this level sometimes give carelessly or disrespectfully, with unwholesome states of mind. The Buddha teaches that in the practice of giving, as in all bodily and verbal conduct, it is the volition accompanying the act that determines its moral quality. If one is offering something to a monk, doing so without adopting a respectful manner would not be proper. Throwing a coin to a beggar in order to get rid of him would also be considered a defilement of giving. One should think carefully about the relevance and the timing of a gift for it to bring the best results. A gift given through an intermediary—for example, having a servant give food to a monk rather than giving it by one's own hand—also detracts from the value of the gift. When one gives without realising that one must experience the results of one's deeds, an act of giving again diminishes in meritorious potency.

If one only plans on giving a donation but does not fulfill one's plan, the merit earned will be very slight. Thus we should always follow up our intentions of generosity expeditiously, unless something intervenes to prevent our doing so. If, after having given a gift, we should subsequently regret our action, much of the merit of the deed will be lost.

A moral person gives politely and respectfully. Whether the gift is spontaneous or planned, he or she will make sure that the timing and contents of the gift are appropriate for the receiver. Many housewives in Buddhist countries regularly invite a few monks to their homes to receive almsfood early in the day. Before feeding the family, these women always offer the food to the bhikkhus with their own hands.

One might contribute to a certain cause from fear that friends would disapprove if one did not give. Giving in response to such social pressure will have weak, though still beneficial, results. Charitable actions undertaken to gain a good reputation are also selfish and hence not a very valuable kind of giving. Nor can it be praiseworthy when one gives merely to return a favour or in expectation of a reward. The former is like repaying a debt, the latter analogous to offering a bribe.

The Recipient of Gifts

The purity of the recipient is another factor which helps determine the kammic fruitfulness of a gift. The worthier the receiver, the greater the benefits that will come to the donor; hence it is good to give to the holiest people available. The Buddha teaches that the worthiest recipients of gifts are the ariyas, the noble ones, such as the Buddha himself and those of his disciples who have reached the supramundane paths and fruits; for it is their purity of mind, attained by wisdom, that makes the act of giving capable of yielding abundant benefits. Therefore, to earn the maximum merit, we should give as much as we can, and as often as possible, to the noble ones. Gifts to a bhikkhu who strives for the state of a noble one, or to a Buddhist meditator who lives by the Five Precepts, will also yield bountiful results.

When ariyas accept offerings, they do so to provide

an opportunity for the donor to earn merit. Non-returners and Arahats in particular, who have attained the two highest stages of sanctity, have eliminated desire for sense objects. Thus when they are given gifts their minds remain detached from the objects presented and are filled with compassion for the giver.

The story of Sīvali in the Dhammapada Commentary[2] is an example of the great merit which even a small gift can yield when presented to the Sangha led by the Buddha. At the time of Vipassī Buddha, the citizens of a country were competing with their king to see who could make the greatest offering to the Buddha and Sangha. The citizens had obtained everything for their offering except fresh honey, and they sent out several messengers, each with plenty of money, to buy the missing ingredient.

One of these men met a villager who happened to be bringing a newly harvested honeycomb into the city for sale. The messenger was only able to buy it from the peasant when he had offered his entire allowance of a thousand pieces of money, which was far more than a single honeycomb was worth. The villager said: "Are you crazy? . . . This honey isn't worth a farthing but you offer me a thousand pieces of money for it. What is the explanation for this?" The other man told him that the honey was worth so much to him because it was the final item on the menu for the citizens' offering to the Buddha. The

---

2. E.W. Burlingame, trans. *Buddhist Legends* (London: Pali Text Society, 1969), 2:212–16.

peasant spontaneously replied, "If that is the case, I will not sell it to you for a price; if I may receive the merit of the offering, I will give it to you." The citizens were impressed with the faith of this man who so readily gave up a windfall and enthusiastically agreed that he should receive the merit of the offering.

Because of this simple gift at the time of Vipassī Buddha, the villager was reborn numerous times in celestial planes and then became the prince who inherited the throne of Benares. In his final lifetime, he became the Elder Sīvali and attained Arahatship as a disciple of the present Buddha. Even after that, his gift of the honeycomb continued to bear fruit. To honour the one who had made the sweet gift aeons before, the gods provided lodging and food for the Buddha and five hundred of his monks, including Sīvali, when for several days they had been walking along a deserted road.

The practice of giving is also beneficial when directed to someone who is not spiritually advanced. If the donor's intention is good, then even though the receiver is immoral, the donor will earn merit and further, by his act of giving, he will strengthen within himself his own disposition to renunciation. A gift mentally offered to the noble Sangha but physically presented to a monk who is morally corrupt will still bear great fruit. To be sure, we should not pretend that a bad person is good, but we must be most careful of our own attitude while giving, as our attitude is the factor over which we have most control.

The Objects to be Given

The third factor involved in giving is the gift itself, which can be either material or immaterial. *Dhamma-dāna*, the gift of the noble teaching, is said by the Buddha to excel all other gifts (Dhammapada, 354). Those who expound his teachings—monks who preach sermons or recite from the Tipiṭika, teachers of meditation—frequently share the Truth, thus practising the highest kind of generosity. Those of us who are not qualified to teach the Dhamma can give the gift of the Dhamma in other ways. We can donate Dhamma books or pay for the translation or publication of a rare or new manuscript propagating the Buddha-Word. We can discuss the Dhamma informally and encourage others to keep precepts or to take up meditation. We might write an explanation of some aspect of the Dhamma for the benefit of others. Giving cash or labour to a meditation centre or helping support a meditation teacher can also be considered the gift of the Dhamma, as the purpose of the centre and the teacher is the transmission of the Buddha's teaching.

The most common type of gift is material things. A material object need not have a high monetary value for it to bring great results, as the story of Sīvali and the honeycomb illustrates. If a poor man gives a monk the cup of rice that was to be his only food for the day, the man is making a great donation which may bear abundant fruit, while if a prosperous merchant, knowing in advance that the monk was coming for alms, were to give the same small portion of rice, he would reap meagre fruits. We should try to give things whose quality is at least as good as those we use ourselves, like the people in Burma, who buy the best fruits on the market as gifts for the monks although these fruits are much too expensive for them to consume themselves.

Gifts to the Sangha may consist of food, robes, medicine or monasteries, each of which has a wide range. The limits are set by the rules of the Vinaya which the Buddha established, as and when required, to keep the Bhikkhu Sangha pure and strong. Lay people who understand the monks' rules can earn vast merit by donating the proper things at the proper time to the order of monks and nuns.

A story about Visākhā, the Buddha's chief woman lay disciple, offers a delightful illustration of the results of large-scale charity.[3] When Visākhā was to be married, elaborate preparations and gifts were arranged by her father. He gave her five hundred cart-loads each of money, of gold, silver and copper vessels, of silk clothes, of ghee and rice, and of farm implements. Then he decided that she must also take cattle with her. He gave orders to his men to allow out of their pen just as many animals as would fill a particular lane. When the cows had filed out and stood close together in that road, he had the corral closed, saying, "These cattle are enough for my daughter." However, after the gate had been latched securely, powerful bulls and milk cows jumped over the barrier to join the animals going with Visākhā. Her father's servants could not keep them inside no matter how hard they tried.

---

3. *Buddhist Legends*, 2:67–68.

All these cattle came to Visākhā because, in a former lifetime long ago at the time of the Buddha Kassapa, she had given a generous gift of five kinds of dairy products to a company of 20,000 monks and novices. As the youngest of the seven daughters of King Kiki of Benares, she continued to urge the monks to take more milk, curds, ghee, etc., even when they said they had eaten enough. That gift earned her the merit of having such a large number of cattle go along with her at her marriage in the lifetime when she was Visākhā, and no one could prevent this merit from bearing its fruit.

Material gifts of a religious nature would include contributions towards the erection of a new temple or shrine, gold leaf to help gild the umbrella of a shrine, or the purchase of a Buddha statue for a temple. The recipients of such gifts are the general public—whoever comes to the temple or worships before the Buddha image.

Mundane gifts to the citizens of one's town would include donations to various welfare organizations, a contribution to a hospital or public library, keeping a neighbourhood park neat and clean. If one does not merely contribute funds for such projects but provides physical labour as well, the kammic results will be even greater. Gifts of this sort can be quite meritorious if preceded, accompanied and followed by pure mental volitions.

The Perfection of Giving

There is a mode of giving which completely disregards the qualities of the recipient and even the mundane fruits of the merit acquired by giving. Such generosity springs from the motive of renunciation, the thought of eliminating one's attachment to one's possessions, and thus aims at giving away the dearest and most difficult gifts. Bodhisattas give in this manner whenever the opportunity presents itself, strictly in order to fulfill the *dānapārami*, the "perfection of giving," which is the first of the ten perfections they must cultivate to the highest degree in order to attain Buddhahood. A Bodhisatta's work to complete the perfection of giving demands much more of him than other beings could emulate. Many Jātaka tales relate how the Bodhisatta who was to become the Buddha Gotama gave things away with absolutely no thought of himself or of the mundane benefits that might follow. A Bodhisatta's only concern in practising generosity is to fulfill the requirements for Buddhahood.

The *Basket of Conduct*[4] contains ten stories of the Bodhisatta's former lives. In one of these lifetimes, he was a brahmin named Sankha who saw a Paccekabuddha, or non-teaching enlightened one, walking barefoot on a desert path. Sankha thought to himself, "Desiring merit, seeing one eminently worthy of a gift of faith, if I do not give him a gift, I will dwindle in merit." So the brahmin, who had a very delicate constitution, presented his sandals to the Paccekabuddha even though his own need for them was greater (Division I, Story 2).

---

4. Cariyāpiṭaka, translated by I. B. Horner, included in *Minor Anthologies of the Pali Canon*, Part III (London: Pali Text Society, 1975).

Another time the Bodhisatta was a great emperor named Mahā-Sudassana. He had criers proclaim several times every day, in thousands of places throughout his empire, that anyone who wanted anything would be given it if he just came there and asked. "If there came a mendicant beggar, whether by day or by night, receiving whatever goods he wanted, he went away with hands full." Mahā-Sudassana gave with completely open-handed generosity, "without attachment, expecting nothing in return, for the attainment of Self-Awakening" (I, 4).

A Bodhisatta must give more difficult gifts than material goods to fulfill the highest form of the perfection of generosity. He must freely give the parts of his body, his children, his wife, and even his own life. As King Sivi, our Bodhisatta plucked out both his eyes with his bare hands and gave them to Sakka, the king of the gods. Sakka had come to Sivi in the guise of a blind old man, just to provide him with the opportunity to make this remarkable gift. Sivi did this with no hesitation prior to the act, nor with any reluctance during the act, nor with any hint of regret afterwards. He said that this gift was made "for the sake of Awakening itself. The two eyes were not disagreeable to me. Omniscience was dear to me, therefore I gave the eyes" (I, 8).

As Prince Vessantara, the Bodhisatta gave the auspicious, powerful royal elephant to the people of a rival kingdom merely because they had requested it. As a result of this liberality, he and his wife and two small children were banished to a remote mountain. They lived there in the forest, Vessantara tending his son and daughter in their hut while his wife spent the days gathering the wild fruits on which they lived. One day a traveller chanced by and asked the Bodhisatta to give him the children. Vessantara gave them away without any hesitation at all. Later he gave away his virtuous wife too. "Neither child was disagreeable to me, the Lady Maddī was not disagreeable. Omniscience was dear to me, therefore I gave away those who were dear" (I,9). It should be noted that at that time, a man's children and wife were generally considered his property. Ages before, the Lady Maddī had aspired to be the wife of the Bodhisatta and to share whatever trials he had to undergo along the path to Buddhahood. The result of her own kamma complemented Prince Vessantara's volition and led to her being given away. Their children must also have been experiencing the results of their own past deeds when they had to leave their parents.

Another time the Bodhisatta took birth as a wise hare. That existence came to an end when, joyously, he jumped into a fire after inviting a famished brahmin (again, Sakka in disguise) to eat him roasted. Because of the purity of the Bodhisatta's mind while making this highest gift of his entire body and life, the blazing fire did not hurt him as it burned his flesh. In relating the story he said that, in fact, the fire had calmed him and brought him peace as if it had been cool water, because he had accomplished the complete perfection of giving.

The Ultimate Goal of Giving

The goal of the Buddhist path is emancipation from

the suffering of repeated existence in saṁsāra. The Buddha taught that uprooting ignorance and the mental defilements it nurtures will bring us to Nibbāna, the utter cessation of suffering. Unwholesome mental tendencies make us cling to what we mistakenly take to be our "selves," they keep us struggling to satisfy our insatiable sense desires with objects that are inherently transitory and thus unsatisfying.

The Buddha said that the practice of giving will aid us in our efforts to purify the mind. Generous gifts accompanied by wholesome volition help to eradicate suffering in three ways. First, when we decide to give something of our own to someone else, we simultaneously reduce our attachment to the object; to make a habit of giving can thus gradually weaken the mental factor of craving, one of the main causes of unhappiness. Second, giving accompanied by wholesome volition will lead to happy future births in circumstances favourable to encountering and practising the pure Buddha Dhamma. Third, and most important, when giving is practised with the intention that the mind becomes pliant enough for the attainment of Nibbāna, the act of generosity will help us develop virtue, concentration and wisdom (*sīla, samādhi, paññā*) right in the present. These three stages make up the Buddha's Noble Eightfold Path, and perfecting the path leads to the extinction of suffering.

If we give in the hope of winning luxury in future lives, we may attain our aim providing that we adhere to the principles of virtuous conduct. According to the Buddha, however, the motivation of working for liberation is far superior to that of aiming at mundane happiness in future births. This is because a gift made with the desire for pleasure is accompanied in part by the unwholesome psychological root craving (*taṇhā*). The merits earned by such gifts are exhausted in transient pleasure, and such mundane happiness keeps us revolving in the round of rebirth, which in the deepest sense is always *dukkha*, subject to suffering. Giving associated with craving cannot contribute to the one form of happiness that does not perish, release from the round, which comes only with the full elimination of craving. Gifts untainted by craving and attachment can only be made during a Buddha Sāsana, the period when the teachings of a Buddha are available. So when we give now, during such a time, we should do so with the aim of putting an end to craving. With the end of craving, suffering ceases, and that is liberation.

May the merits of this gift
of the Dhamma
be shared by all beings!

GIVING IN THE PALI CANON

Lily de Silva

Dāna, giving, is extolled in the Pali Canon as a great virtue. It is, in fact, the beginning of the path to liberation. When the Buddha preaches to a newcomer he starts his graduated sermon with an exposition on the virtues of giving (*dānakathā*, Vin.i,15, 18). Of the three bases for the performance of meritorious deeds (*puññakiriyavatthu*), giving is the first, the other two being virtue and mental culture (A.iv,241). It is also the first of the ten *pāramitā* perfected by a Buddha. Therefore, on the march towards liberation as an Arahant or a Buddha, one initially has to practise *dāna*.

Function of Giving

Giving is of prime importance in the Buddhist scheme of mental purification because it is the best weapon against greed (*lobha*), the first of the three unwholesome motivational roots (*akusalamūla*). Greed is wrapt up with egoism and selfishness, since we hold our personalities and our possessions as "I" and "mine." Giving helps make egoism thaw: it is the antidote to cure the illness of egoism and greed. "Overcome the taint of greed and practise giving," exhorts the Devatāsaṁyutta (S.i,18). The Dhammapada admonishes us to conquer miserliness with generosity (*jine kadariyaṁ dānena*, Dhp. 223).

It is difficult to exercise this virtue of giving proportionate to the intensity of one's greed and selfishness. As such the Devatāsaṁyutta equates giving to a battle (*dānañ ca yuddhañ ca samānam āhu*, S. i,20). One has to fight the evil forces of greed before one can make up one's mind to give away something dear and useful to oneself. The Laṭukikopama Sutta illustrates how a man lacking in spiritual strength finds it hard to give up a thing he has been used to (M.i,449). A small quail can come to death when it gets entangled even in a useless rotten creeper. Though weak, a rotten creeper is a great bond for the small bird. But even an iron chain is not too big a bond for a strong elephant. Similarly, a poor wretched man of weak character would find it difficult to part with his shabby meagre belongings, while a strong charactered king will even give up a kingdom once convinced of the dangers of greed.

Miserliness is not the only hindrance to giving. Carelessness and ignorance of the working of kamma and survival after death are equally valid causes (*maccherā ca pamādā ca evaṁ dānaṁ na dīyati*, S.i,18). If one knows the moral advantages of giving, one will be vigilant to seize opportunities to practise this great virtue. Once the Buddha said that if people only knew the value of giving as he does, they would not take a single meal without sharing their food with others (It. p. 18).

Qualities of the Donor

The suttas (e.g. D.i,137) employ a number of terms to describe the qualities of a donor. He is a man with faith (*saddhā*), he has faith in the nobility of a morally sound life, in the teachings of kamma and survival after death. He believes in the possibility of the moral and spiritual perfection of man. In short, he is not a materialist, and he has faith in the Buddha, the Dhamma and the Sangha. He is not merely a giver (*dāyako*), he is a lordly giver (*dānapati*). The commentary explains the concept of "lordly giver" in the following words: "He who himself enjoys delicious things but gives to others what is not delicious is a donor who is a slave to the gifts he gives. He who gives things of the same quality as he himself enjoys is one who is like a friend of the gift. He who satisfies himself with whatever he can get but gives delicacies to others is a lordly giver, a senior and a master of the gifts given."

The donor is also described as one who keeps an open house for the needy (*anāvaṭadvāro*). He is like a wellspring (*opānabhūto*) for recluses, brahmins, the destitute, wayfarers, wanderers and beggars. Being such a one he does meritorious deeds. He is munificent (*muttacāgo*) and is interested in sharing his blessings with others (*dānasaṁvibhāgarato*). He is a philanthropist who understands the difficulties of the poor (*vadaññū*). He is open-handed and is ready to comply with another's request (*payatapāṇī*). He is one fit to be asked from (*yācayogo*). He takes delight in distributing gifts to the needy (*vossaggarato*), and has a heart bent on giving (*cāgaparibhāvitacitto*). Such are the epithets used in the suttas to describe the qualities of the liberal-minded.

A noble giver is one who is happy before, during

and after giving (A.iii,336). Before giving he is happy anticipating the opportunity to exercise his generosity. While giving he is happy that he is making another happy by fulfilling a need. After giving he is satisfied that he has done a good deed. The suttas list generosity as one of the important qualities that go to make a gentleman (A.iv,220). The Buddha compares the man who righteously earns his wealth and gives of it to the needy to a man who has both eyes, whereas the one who only earns wealth but does no merit is like a one-eyed man (A.i,129-30). The wealthy man who enjoys his riches by himself without sharing is said to be digging his own grave (Sn. 102).

The Donations

Practically anything useful can be given as a gift. The Niddesa (Nd.2, 523) gives a list of fourteen items that are fit to be given for charity. They are robes, almsfood, dwelling places, medicine and other requisites for the sick, food, drink, cloths, vehicles, garlands, perfume, unguent, beds, houses and lamps. It is not necessary to have much to practise generosity, for one can give according to one's means. Gifts given from one's meagre resources are considered very valuable (*appasmā dakkhiṇā dinnā sahassena samaṁ mitā*, S.i,18; *dajjāppasmim pi yācito*, Dhp. 224). If a person leads a righteous life even though he ekes out a bare existence on gleanings, looks after his family according to his means, but makes it a point to give from his limited stores, his generosity is worth more than a thousand sacrifices (S.i,19-20). Alms given from wealth righteously earned is greatly praised by the Buddha (A.iii,354; It. p. 66; A.iii,45-46). A householder who does so is said to be one who is lucky here and hereafter. In the Māgha Sutta of the Sutta Nipāta (Sn.p.87) the Buddha highly appreciates Māgha who says that he earns through righteous means and liberally gives of it to the needy.

Even if one gives a small amount with a heart full of faith one can gain happiness hereafter. The Vimānavattha supplies ample examples. According to the Ācāmadāyikāvimānavatthu, the alms given consisted of a little rice crust, but as it was given with great devotion to an eminent Arahant, the reward was rebirth in a magnificent celestial mansion. The Dakkhiṇāvibhanga Sutta states that an offering is purified on account of the giver when the giver is virtuous, on account of the recipient when the recipient is virtuous, on account of both the giver and the recipient if both are virtuous, by none if both happen to be impious. *Dhammadāna*, the dissemination of the knowledge of the Dhamma, is said to excel all other forms of giving (*sabbadānaṁ dhammadānaṁ jināti*, Dhp. 354).

The Anguttara Nikāya mentions five great gifts which have been held in high esteem by noble-minded men from ancient times (A.iv,246). Their value was not doubted in ancient times, it is not doubted at present, nor will it be doubted in the future. The wise recluses and brahmins had the highest respect for them. These great givings comprise the meticulous observance of the Five Precepts. By doing so one gives fearlessness, love and benevolence to all beings. If one human being can give security and freedom from fear to others by his behaviour, that is the highest form of *dāna* one can give, not only to mankind, but to all living beings.

The Donee

The suttas also describe the person to whom alms should be given (A.iii,41). Guests, travellers and the sick should be treated with hospitality and due consideration. During famines the needy should be liberally entertained. The virtuous should be first entertained with the first fruits of fresh crops. There is a recurrent phrase in the suttas (D.i,137; ii,354; iii,76) describing those who are particularly in need of public generosity. They are recluses (*samaṇa*), brahmins (*brāhmaṇa*), destitutes (*kapaṇa*), wayfarers (*addhika*), wanderers (*vaṇibbaka*) and beggars (*yācaka*). The recluses and brahmins are religious persons who do not earn wages. They give spiritual guidance to the laity and the laity is expected to support them. The poor need the help of the rich to survive and the rich become spiritually richer by helping the poor. At a time when transport facilities were meagre and amenities for travellers were not adequately organised, the public had to step in to help the wayfarer. Buddhism considers it a person's moral obligation to give assistance to all these types of people.

In the Anguttara Nikāya the Buddha describes, with sacrificial terminology, three types of fires that should be tended with care and honour (A.iv,44). They are *āhuneyyaggi*, *gahapataggi* and *dakkhiṇeyyaggi*. The Buddha explained that *āhuneyyaggi* means one's parents, and they should be honoured and cared for.

Gahapataggi means one's wife and children, employees and dependents. *Dakkhiṇeyyaggi* represents religious persons who have either attained the goal of Arahantship or have embarked on a course of training for the elimination of negative mental traits. All these should be cared for and looked after as one would tend a sacrificial fire. According to the Mahāmangala Sutta, offering hospitality to one's relatives is one of the great auspicious deeds a layperson can perform (Sn. 262-63).

King Kosala once asked the Buddha to whom alms should be given (S.i,98). The Buddha replied that alms should be given to those by giving to whom one becomes happy. Then the king asked another question: To whom should alms be offered to obtain great fruit? The Buddha discriminated the two as different questions and replied that alms offered to the virtuous bears great fruit. He further clarified that offerings yield great fruit when made to virtuous recluses who have eliminated the five mental hindrances (*nīvaraṇa*) and cultivated moral habits, concentration, wisdom, emancipation and knowledge and vision of emancipation (*sīla, samādhi, paññā, vimutti, vimuttiñāṇadassana*).

In the Sakkasaṁyutta (S.i,233) Sakka asked the same question from the Buddha: Gifts given to whom bring the greatest results? The Buddha replied that what is given to the Sangha bears great results. Here the Buddha specifies that what he means by "Sangha" is the community of those upright noble individuals who have entered the path and who have established themselves in the fruit of saintship, and who are endowed with morality, concentration and wisdom. It is important to note that "Sangha" according to the Vinaya means a sufficient group of monks to represent the Order of monks for various ecclesiastical purposes (Vin.i,319). But in the suttas "Sangha" means the four pairs of noble individuals or the eight particular individuals (*cattāri purisayugāni, aṭṭha purisapuggalā*), i.e. those who are on the path to stream-entry, once-returning, non-returning, and Arahantship, and those who have obtained the fruits thereof.

The Māgha Sutta (Sn. p. 86) gives a detailed account of the virtues of the Arahant to show to whom alms should be offered by one desiring merit. The Brāhmaṇasaṁyutta (S.i,175) maintains that offerings bear greatest results when they are made to those who know their previous lives, who have seen heavens and hells, who have put an end to birth and who have realized ultimate knowledge. Thus the Sangha comprising morally perfect, worthy personages as described in the suttas constitutes the field of merit (*puññakkhetta*, M.i,447). Just as seeds sown in fertile well-watered fields yield bountiful crops, alms given to the virtuous established on the Noble Eightfold Path yield great results (A.iv,238; i,162). The Dhammapada maintains that fields have weeds as their blemish; lust, hatred, delusion and desire are the blemishes of people, and therefore what is given to those who have eliminated those blemishes bears great fruit (Dhp. 356-59). The results of generosity are measured more by the quality of the field of merit represented by the recipient than by the quantity and value of the gift given.

The Anguttara Nikāya (A.iv,392–95) records a fabulous alms-giving conducted by the Bodhisatta when he was born as a brahmin named Velāma. Lavish gifts of silver, gold, elephants, cows, carriages, etc., not to mention food, drink and clothing, were distributed among everybody who came forward to receive them. But this open-handed munificence was not very valuable as far as merit was concerned because there were no worthy recipients. It is said to be more meritorious to feed one person with right view, a stream-enterer (*sotāpanna*), than to give great alms such as that given by Velāma. It is more meritorious to feed one once-returner than a hundred stream-enterers. Next in order come non-returners, Arahants, Paccekabuddhas and Sammāsambuddhas. Feeding the Buddha and the Sangha is more meritorious than feeding the Buddha alone. It is even more meritorious to construct a monastery for the general use of the Sangha of the four quarters of all times. Taking refuge in the Buddha, Dhamma and Sangha is better still. Abiding by the Five Precepts is even more valuable. But better still is the cultivation of *mettā*, loving-kindness, and best of all, the insight into impermanence, which leads to Nibbāna.

The Motivation for Giving

The *suttas* record various motives for exercising generosity. The Anguttara Nikāya (A.iv,236) enumerates the following eight motives:

1. *Āsajja dānaṁ deti:* one gives with annoyance, or as a way of offending the recipient, or with the

idea of insulting him.[1]

2. *Bhayā dānaṁ deti:* fear also can motivate a person to make an offering.

3. *Adāsi me ti dānaṁ deti:* one gives in return for a favour done to oneself in the past.

4. *Dassati me ti dānaṁ deti:* one also may give with the hope of getting a similar favour for oneself in the future.

5. *Sādhu dānan ti dānaṁ deti:* one gives because giving is considered good.

6. *Ahaṁ pacāmi, ime ne pacanti, na arahāmi pacanto apacantānaṁ adātun ti dānaṁ deti:* "I cook, they do not cook. It is not proper for me who cook not to give to those who do not cook." Some give urged by such altruistic motives.

7. *Imaṁ me dānaṁ dadato kalyāṇo kittisaddo abbhuggacchatī ti dānaṁ deti:* some give alms to gain a good reputation.

8. *Cittālankāra-cittaparikkhāratthaṁ dānaṁ deti:* still others give alms to adorn and beautify the mind.

Favouritism (*chanda*), ill will (*dosa*) and delusion (*moha*) are also listed as motives for giving. Sometimes alms are given for the sake of maintaining a long-standing family tradition. Desire to be reborn in

---

1. Though the PTS translation reads "one gives alms on one's own accord," the accuracy of this translation is questionable. The sutta seems to record motives for giving in ascending order of refinement. If the PTS translation is accepted, the order is disturbed. Moreover, *āsajja* is the gerund of *āsādeti*, which means to strike, offend, assail, insult.

heaven after death is another dominant motive. Giving pleases some and they give with the idea of winning a happy frame of mind (A.iv,236).

But it is maintained in the suttas (A.iv,62) that alms should be given without any expectations (*na sāpekho dānaṁ deti*). Nor should alms be given with attachment to the recipient. If one gives with the idea of accumulating things for later use, that is an inferior act of giving. If one gives with the hope of enjoying the result thereof after death, that is also an inferior act of giving. The only valid motive for giving should be the motive of adorning the mind, to rid the mind of the ugliness of greed and selfishness.

The Manner of Giving

The suttas (e.g. A.iii,172) lay much emphasis on the manner of giving. The attitude of the donor in the act of giving makes a world of difference for the goodwill between the donor and recipient irrespective of whether the gift given is big or small. *Sakkaccaṁ dānaṁ deti:* alms should be given in such a way that the donee does not feel humiliated, belittled or hurt. The needy ask for something with a sense of embarrassment, and it is the duty of the donor not to make him feel more embarrassed and make his already heavy burden still heavier. *Cittikatvā dānaṁ deti:* alms should be given with due consideration and respect. The recipient should be made to feel welcome. It is when a gift is given with such warmth that a cohesive mutually enriching friendliness emerges between the donor and donee. *Sahatthā deti:* one should give with one's own hand. The personal involvement in the act of giving is greatly beneficial. This promotes rapport between the donor and donee and that is the social value of giving. Society is welded in unity with care and concern for one another when generosity is exercised with a warm sense of personal involvement. *Na apaviddhaṁ deti:* one should not give as alms what is only fit to be thrown away. One should be careful to give only what is useful and appropriate. *Na anāgamanadiṭṭhiko deti:* one should not give in such a callous manner so as to make the donee not feel like coming again.

Giving with faith (*saddhāya deti*) is much extolled in the suttas (A.iii,172). Especially when offering alms to the clergy one should do so with due deference and respect, taking delight in the opportunity one has got to serve them. One should also give at the proper time to meet a dire need (*kālena deti*). Such timely gifts are most valuable as they relieve the anxiety and stress of the suppliant. One should give with altruistic concerns, with the sole intention of helping another in difficulty (*anuggahacitto dānaṁ deti*). In the act of giving one should take care not to hurt oneself or another (*attānañ ca parañ ca anupahacca dānaṁ deti*). Giving with understanding and discretion is praised by the Buddha (*viceyyadānaṁ sugatappasatthaṁ*). If a gift contributes to the well-being of the donee it is wise to give. But if the gift is detrimental to the welfare of the donee one should be careful to exercise one's discretion. Giving as described above is highly commended as noble giving (*sappurisadāna*). More than what is given, it is the manner of giving that makes a gift valuable. One may not be able to afford a lavish gift, but one can always make the recipient feel cared for by the manner of giving.

The Value of Giving

Many suttas enumerate the various benefits of giving. Giving promotes social cohesion and solidarity. It is the best means of bridging the psychological gap, much more than the material economic gap, that exists between haves and have-nots. The Magha Sutta maintains that hate gets eliminated when one is established in generosity (Sn. 506). The one with a generous heart earns the love of others and many associate with him (A.iii,40). Giving also cements friendships (Sn. 187).

It is maintained that if a person makes an aspiration to be born in a particular place after giving alms, the aspiration will be fulfilled only if he is virtuous, but not otherwise (A.iv,239). According to one sutta (A.iv,241-43), if one practises giving and morality to a very limited degree and has no idea about meditation, one obtains an unfortunate birth in the human world. One who performs meritorious deeds such as giving and morality to a considerable degree, but does not understand anything about meditation, meets a fortunate human birth. But those who practise giving and morality to a great extent without any knowledge of meditation find rebirth in one of the heavens. They excel other deities in the length of life, beauty, pleasure, fame and the five strands of sense pleasures.

The Anguttara Nikāya (A.iv,79) enumerates a number of this-worldly benefits of giving. The generous peson, and not the miser, wins the sympathy of others. Arahants approach him, accept alms and preach to him first. A good reputation spreads about him. He can attend any assembly with confidence and dignity. He is reborn in a state of happiness after death. Another sutta (A.iii,41) adds that a generous person wins popularity; people of noble character associate with him and he has the satisfaction of having fulfilled a layperson's duties (*gihidhammā anapeto hoti*).

It is said that an almsgiver bestows on others life, beauty, happiness, strength and intelligence. Having bestowed them on others, he becomes a beneficiary of them himself (A.iii,42). The same idea is expressed by the succinct statement that one reaps what one sows (*yādisaṁ vapate bījaṁ tādisaṁ harate phalaṁ*, S.i,227).

Giving with faith results in the attainment of riches and beauty whenever the fruition of the gift occurs. By giving alms with due deference one gains, in addition, children, wives, subordinates and servants who are obedient, dutiful and understanding. By giving alms at the proper time not only does one obtain great wealth but also timely fulfilment of needs. By giving alms with the genuine desire to help others, one gains great wealth and the inclination to enjoy the best of sense pleasures. By giving alms without hurting oneself and others, one gains security from dangers such as fire, floods, thieves, kings and unloved heirs (A.iii,172).

Alms given to recluses and brahmins who follow the Noble Eightfold Path yield wonderful results just as seeds sown on fertile, well-prepared, well-watered fields produce abundant crops (A.iv,238). Alms given without any expectations whatsoever can lead to birth in the Brahma-world, at the end of which one may become a non-returner (A.iv,62).

The Dakkhiṇāvibhanga Sutta enumerates a list of persons to whom alms can be offered and the merit accruing therefrom in ascending order. A thing given to an animal brings a reward a hundredfold. A gift given to an ordinary person of poor moral habit yields a reward a thousandfold; a gift given to a virtuous person yields a reward a hundred thousandfold. When a gift is given to a person outside the dispensation of Buddhism who is without attachment to sense pleasures, the yield is a hundred thousandfold of crores. When a gift is given to one on the path to stream-entry the yield is incalculable and immeasurable. So what can be said of a gift given to a stream-enterer, a once-returner, a non-returner, an Arahant, a Paccekabuddha, and a Fully Enlightened Buddha?

The same sutta emphasizes that a gift given to the Sangha as a group is more valuable than a gift offered to a single monk in his individual capacity. It is said that in the distant future there will be Buddhist monks who wear only a yellow collar as a distinguishing clerical mark, who are immoral and of evil character. If a gift is offered even to such monks in the name of the Order, it yields much more merit than a gift given to a monk in his individual capacity. But it should be observed that this statement is contradictory to ideas expressed elsewhere, that what is given to the virtuous is greatly beneficial but not what is given to the immoral. It is evident here that a later interpolation cannot be altogether ruled out.

The Buddha once explained that it is a meritorious act even to throw away the water after washing one's plate with the generous thought: "May the particles of food in the washing water be food to the creatures on the ground." When that is so, how much more meritorious it is to feed a human being! But the sutta hastens to add that it is more meritorious to feed a virtuous person (A.i,161).

Another sutta (A.iii,336) maintains that it is not possible to estimate the amount of merit that accrues when an offering is endowed with six particular characteristics. Three of the characteristics belong to the donor while three belong to the donee. The donor should be happy at the thought of giving prior to making the offering. He should be pleased at the time of making the offering, and he should be satisfied after the offering is made. Thus the nobility of thought—without a trace of greed before, during and after the offering—makes a gift truly great. The recipients also should be free from lust, hatred and delusion, or they should have embarked on a course of training for the elimination of these mental depravities. When an almsgiving is endowed with these qualities of the donor and donee, the merit is said to be as immeasurable as the waters in the ocean.

Once Visākhā gave a learned explanation of the benefits she expected from her munificence when the Buddha questioned her as to what she saw as the advantages of her great generosity (Vin.i,293-94). She said that when she hears that a particular monk or nun has attained any of the fruits of recluseship, and if that monk or nun has visited Sāvatthī, she would be certain that he or she has partaken of the offerings she constantly makes. When she reflects that she has contributed in some measure to his or her spiritual distinction, great delight (*pāmujja*) arises in her. Joy (*pīti*) arises in the mind that is delighted. When the mind is joyful the body relaxes (*kāyo passambhissati*). When the body relaxes a sense of ease (*sukha*) is experienced which helps the mind to be concentrated (*cittaṁ samādhiyissati*). That will help the development of the spiritual faculties (*indriyabhāvanā*), spiritual powers (*balabhāvanā*), and factors of enlightenment (*bojjhangabhāvanā*). These are the advantages she hopes for by her munificence. The Buddha was so pleased with her erudite reply that he exclaimed "*Sādhu sādhu sādhu*" in approbation.

It is evident that giving alone is not sufficient for one to make an end of suffering. Anāthapiṇḍika, who was pronounced by the Buddha as the foremost among almsgivers, became only a stream-enterer. It is specifically said that *dāna* has to be fortified by *sīla*, morality, if it is to produce good results. Though Anāthapiṇḍika practised unblemished virtue, it is nowhere stated that he practised mental culture or meditation (*bhāvanā*). Therefore, in spite of all his magnanimous munificence, he had to remain a stream-enterer.

The *Ghaṭīkāra Sutta* (M.ii,52) records a unique almsgiving where even the donor was not present. Ghaṭīkāra the potter was the chief benefactor of the Buddha Kassapa. He was a non-returner who did not want to enter the Order as he was looking after his blind, aged parents. He had greatly won the trust of the Buddha by the nobility of his conduct and devotion. One day the Buddha Kassapa went to his house on his alms round but Ghaṭīkāra was out. He asked the blind parents where the potter had gone. They replied that he had gone out, but invited the Buddha to serve himself from the pots and pans and partake of a meal. The Buddha did so. When Ghaṭīkāra returned and inquired who had taken from the food, the parents informed him that the Buddha had come and they had requested him to help himself to a meal. Ghaṭīkāra was overjoyed to hear this as he felt that the Buddha had so much trust in him. It is said that the joy and happiness (*pītisukha*) he experienced did not leave him for two weeks, and the parents' joy and happiness did not wane for a whole week.

The same sutta reports that on another occasion the roof of the Buddha Kassapa's monastery started leaking. He sent the monks to Ghaṭīkāra's house to fetch some straw, but Ghaṭīkāra was out at that time. Monks came back and said that there was no straw available there except what was on the roof. The Buddha asked the monks to get the straw from the roof there. Monks started stripping the straw from the roof and the aged parents of Ghaṭīkāra asked who was removing the straw. The monks explained the matter and the parents said, "Please do take all the straw." When Ghaṭīkāra heard about this he was deeply moved by the trust the Buddha reposed in him. The joy and happiness that arose in him did not leave him for a full fortnight and that of his parents did not subside for a week. For three months Ghaṭīkāra's house remained without a roof with only the sky above, but it is said that the rain did not wet the house. Such was the great piety and generosity of Ghaṭīkāra.

As mentioned at the beginning of this essay, *dāna* is the first of the meritorious deeds. It is also one of the four benevolent ways of treating others (*cattāri sangahavatthūni*, A.iv,219). But it is noteworthy that in the lists of virtues required for liberation such as those included among the thirty-seven requisites of enlightenment (*bodhipakkhiyā dhammā*), *dāna* never occurs as a required virtue. Instead of *dāna, cāga* or generosity is included in some of the lists, such as the five qualities—faith, virtue, learning, generosity and wisdom. Perhaps there is a slight difference between *dāna* and *cāga* when considered as virtues ingrained in the mind. *Dāna* is the very practical act of giving, *cāga* is the generous attitude ingrained in the mind by the repeated practice of *dāna*. The word *cāga* literally means giving up, abandonment, and it is an indication that the close-fisted selfish grip one has on one's possessions is loosened by *cāga*. It is possible to give alms even out of negative motives such as favouritism (*chanda*), ill will (*dosa*), fear (*bhaya*), delusion (*moha*), desire for a good reputation, etc., but *cāga* is the positive virtue of a generous disposition.

Buddhism teaches a gradual process of emptying oneself. It starts with giving away one's external possessions. When the generous dispositional trait sets in and is fortified by the deepening insight into the real nature of things, one grows disenchanted with sense pleasures (*nibbindati*). At this stage one gives up household life and seeks ordination. Next comes the emptying of sensory inputs by guarding the sense doors. Through meditation (*bhāvanā*) one empties oneself of deep-seated defilements and fills oneself with positive noble qualities. But this whole process of bailing out negativities starts with *dāna*, the practice of giving.

GIVING FROM THE HEART

M. O'C. Walshe

Giving comes very naturally to some people—they enjoy giving and are unhappy if they cannot do so. And though it is obvious that one can give foolishly, it is in general a very good and meritorious thing to give. This is recognized in, probably, all religions: in Christianity we are told that it is more blessed to give than to receive, and in Islam there is a positive injunction to give part of one's wealth to the poor.

Perhaps, however, we ought to start by squarely facing a point which may worry some people: the question of giving to the Sangha. In a phrase which lay Buddhists may frequently hear chanted, or even chant themselves, the Sangha is described as *anuttaraṁ puññakkhettaṁ lokassa*, "an unequalled field of merit-making for the world," meaning that the merit to be gained by giving to the Sangha is unequalled. Well of course, not all the lay people who hear or join in such chanting know what the words mean, but of those who do, Westerners who are Buddhists or Buddhist sympathizers sometimes react to this notion with a degree of indignation, considering the words tactless or worse! In fact some, whose conditioning was at least partly under the influence of the Lutheran Christian tradition, are reminded of the abuses to which Martin Luther objected in the Church of his day, when "good deeds" were very largely associated in the popular mind with maintaining priests and monks, who in some cases at least were idle and corrupt, in the style to which they were accustomed.

Such misgivings are perhaps understandable, but can be countered by a proper explanation, and will in any case not take root provided the Sangha is patently seen to be well conducted (*supaṭipanno*). The traditional Buddhist community consists of four groups: monks, nuns, male and female lay followers. Though the original order of nuns has died out, there are women who have undertaken the holy life and live virtually as nuns, and there is every indication that their numbers will grow. The relation between the first two groups and the latter two is one of symbiosis. After all, the Sangha has a priceless gift to give, the gift of the Dhamma. *Sabbadānaṁ dhammadānaṁ jināti*: "The gift of the Dhamma excels all other gifts" (Dhp. 354). Members of the Sangha also have an inescapable obligation to live according to the Vinaya and to strive continuously for enlightenment. It is in fact only by so doing that they can claim to be "an unequalled field of merit-making," and if they fail in this obligation they are letting down not only themselves but also the laity who support them. A monk or nun who cannot observe the rules should, and in certain cases must, leave the Order. This could be regarded, at least in part, as the price to be paid for abusing the generosity of lay supporters.

It was mentioned above that, according to the Bible, it is more blessed to give than to receive. It is interesting to note that, just as in the practice of *mettā-bhāvanā*, the meditation on universal love, there is given an actual method for fulfilling that difficult Judaeo-Christian injunction "love thy neighbour as thyself," so too Buddhism can give a precise technical meaning to this biblical statement. If we receive something pleasant, this in Buddhism is considered to be *vipāka*, the result of previous meritorious conduct. It is nice while it lasts, but when it is finished, its virtue is exhausted. To give, however, is *kusala kamma*, skilled action, which will be productive of some pleasant *vipāka* or result for the giver. In this way it can be clearly seen to be more "blessed" to give than to receive. True, this "blessing" remains purely mundane and limited, being "merit-making for the world" (*lokassa*). But as all our actions are habit-forming, giving once inclines us to give again, so that the result tends to be cumulative. Also, of course, this kind of *kusala kamma* can lead on to other things, and it is not for nothing that *dāna* is listed as the first among the ten *pāramis* or "perfections," coming even before *sīla* or morality. It is, after all, possible for an immoral person to be generous!

The late Dr. I. B. Horner selected ten Jātaka stories to illustrate the ten perfections, in a little book that is widely used as an introductory Pali reader, and she used the delightful story of the self-sacrificing hare (No. 316) to illustrate the perfection of giving. Strangely enough, though, to the Western mind at least, the most popular Jātaka story on this theme is the very last, the Vessantara Jātaka (No. 547), in which the Bodhisatta gives everything away including, finally, his wife and children—a distinctly dubious moral, one might think! But in Thailand this story has been singled out and is regularly made the subject of special readings and sermons for the edification of the laity.

Giving is something that comes from the heart, and as I have said, there are people who enjoy giving for its own sake—which is fine provided the giving is balanced with wisdom. There are of course other people who are reluctant givers, and they are often the same people who find it difficult to say "please," "thank you," "I'm sorry," and so on. For all such types the *brahmavihāra* meditations on love and compassion would be beneficial, to enable them to open up their hearts.

Recently, in Britain, we have had a magnificent example of the power of giving from the heart, and from what to many must have seemed an unexpected source. Moved by the plight of the starving people in Ethiopia, the rock star Bob Geldof organized the fantastic international Live Aid concert which raised millions of pounds—in its way, and with the aid of modern technology, the most spectacular act of generosity in history, touching the hearts of millions, and transcending the boundaries not only of politics and religions, but also that gulf that exists between those addicted to this particular form of entertainment and those who dislike it.

It is perhaps hardly necessary to point out that *dāna* has to be exercised with discretion, and is as much subject to the rule of the middle way as everything else. It is not the best way to bring up a child, for instance, to give it everything it wants—or thinks it wants. Contrary to some trendy theories recently current, it does no harm to frustrate a spoilt brat occasionally! Nor, of course, is it the highest kind of giving if one expects something in return—even a nice rebirth in some heavenly realm! That is a kind of giving which is basically rooted in attachment and is therefore of limited kammic value.

In point of fact, one of the true benefits to the giver is precisely that the act of spontaneous giving is a very fine way of helping to overcome attachment. And that is the intended point of the Vessantara story. We Westerners think of the unfortunate wife and family the Bodhisatta "sacrificed" (though of course there was a happy ending and they came back to him, in the story!), but the intention is to regard them as objects of attachment, to be given up as such. As a matter of fact, despite the popularity of this particular story, modern scholars consider that it was not originally a Buddhist tale at all, and was somewhat unskilfully adapted to provide a "Buddhist" moral.

The more we consider the question of *dāna,* the more aspects emerge, and we see that there are many ways of giving, skilfully or otherwise. We may conclude with an amusing canonical example of the alleged results of relatively unskilful giving. In the Pāyāsi Sutta (No. 23 of the Dīgha Nikāya) we read of the debate between the skeptic Prince Pāyāsi, who did not believe in an afterlife, and the Venerable Kumāra-Kassapa. After listening to a brilliant series of parables from the monk, Pāyāsi declares himself converted, and decides to establish a charity "for ascetics and brahmins, wayfarers, beggars and the needy," and he appoints the young brahmin Uttara to organize the distribution. (N.B. This is the correct version—there is an error in the Rhys Davids translation at this point.) Uttara complains that the food and clothing he is called upon to distribute are of such poor quality that Pāyāsi would not touch them himself, and Pāyāsi finally gives him leave to supply "food as I eat and clothes as I wear." At the conclusion of the sutta, we are told of the rewards the two men received after death. Pāyāsi, who had established the charity grudgingly, was indeed reborn in a heavenly world, but in the very lowest, that of the Four Great Kings, where he was lodged in the empty Serīsaka mansion (*vimāna*). Here, indeed, he was visited by the Venerable Gavampati, an Arahant who made a habit of taking his siesta in the lower heavens. And so the story was brought back to earth. But Uttara, who had reorganized the charity and given from the heart, was born in a higher heaven, among the Thirty-three Gods.

Probably few Westerners will give in order to be reborn among the Thirty-three Gods, and perhaps the only reward some people look to is an easing of the conscience: being aware of some particular need—of which the case of Ethiopia is the outstanding current example—people feel unable to live with themselves if they do *not* give something. This is certainly better than hoping for a heavenly reward, but an easy conscience, too, may perhaps sometimes be purchased a little too easily. Best let the giving itself be its own reward, and leave it at that!

GENEROSITY: THE INWARD DIMENSION

Nina Van Gorkom

> As from a heap of flowers many a garland is made, even so many good deeds should be done by one born a mortal.
>
> Dhammapada, 53

The giving away of useful or pleasant things is an act of generosity. However, if we only pay attention to the outward deeds we do not know whether or not we are being sincerely generous. We should learn more about the mind which motivates our deeds. True generosity is difficult. While we are giving, our thoughts may not all be good and noble. Our motives for giving may not all be pure. We may give with selfish motives—expecting something in return, hoping to be liked by the receiver of our gift, wanting to be known as a generous person. We may notice that there are different thoughts at different moments, some truly generous, and others having different motives.

The Buddha taught that there is no lasting mind or soul which undergoes different experiences. Our experiences themselves are different moments of consciousness, which arise one at a time and then fall away immediately. Each moment of consciousness that arises and falls away is succeeded by the next moment of consciousness. Our life is thus a series of moments of consciousness arising in succession. Gradually we can learn to distinguish different types of consciousness. There is consciousness which is unwholesome or unskilful, and there is consciousness which is wholesome or skilful, and besides these there are other types of consciousness which are neither wholesome nor unwholesome. Only one type of consciousness occurs at a time, but each type is accompanied by several mental factors. Unwholesome types of consciousness are accompanied by unwholesome mental factors, such as attachment, stinginess, jealousy or aversion. Wholesome types of consciousness are accompanied by beautiful mental factors, such as generosity, kindness or compassion.

Three of the unwholesome mental factors are "roots of evil."[1] These are the strong foundation of unwholesome types of consciousness: attachment or greed, aversion or anger, and ignorance.

Each of these unwholesome factors has many shades and degrees. We may know that there is attachment when we are greedy for food or desire to acquire someone else's property. However, we may not realize that there is also attachment when we enjoy natural scenery or beautiful music. In society attachment of a subtle kind is considered good, provided we do not harm others. The unwholesome has a wider range than what we call in conventional language "immoral." It can include states that are weaker than the immoral. We cannot force ourselves not to

---

1. See Nyanaponika Thera, *The Roots of Good and Evil* (Wheel No. 251/253).

like beautiful things; there are conditions for the arising of attachment. But we can learn to know the difference between the moments which are wholesome and the moments which are unwholesome. A degree of selfishness persists even in moments of subtle attachment. These are different from selfless moments of consciousness accompanied by generosity, when we do not think of our own enjoyment. There is attachment time and again, when we stand up, move around, reach for things, eat or go to sleep. We think of ourselves and want to acquire pleasant things for ourselves. We expect other people to be nice to us, and this is also a form of attachment.

We may wonder whether attachment to relatives is wholesome. Attachment to relatives is not wholesome; it is different from pure loving-kindness, which is wholesome. When we cling to the pleasant feeling we derive from the company of relatives or dear friends, there is attachment. When we are genuinely concerned for someone else we do not think of ourselves, and then there is wholesome consciousness. We are so used to living with attachment that we may have never considered the difference between the moments of attachment and the moments of unselfish love. The different types of consciousness succeed one another so rapidly that so long as we have not developed understanding of them, we do not notice that they have changed.

The unwholesome root of aversion also has many degrees. It can manifest as slight uneasiness or as coarse anger or hate. Aversion does not arise at the same time as attachment. When there is attachment consciousness likes the object that is experienced, and when there is aversion consciousness dislikes the object. Attachment arises with certain types of consciousness, not with all types, and so does aversion.

Ignorance is an unwholesome root that arises with all types of unwholesome consciousnes. It is the root of all evil. Ignorance does not know what is wholesome and what is unwholesome, it does not know anything about what is real. Whenever there is attachment or aversion, at the same time there is also ignorance.

The three beautiful roots are: non-attachment or generosity, non-aversion or kindness, and understanding or wisdom. Each type of wholesome consciousness is rooted in non-attachment and non-aversion, and it may be rooted in understanding as well. Each of these beautiful roots has many degrees. Without the assistance of non-attachment and non-aversion wholesome consciousness could not arise motivating acts of generosity. Attachment cannot exist at the same time as generosity. When one is truly generous one gives impartially and does not restrict one's generosity to people one likes or to the members of one's family. The purpose of all kinds of wholesomeness should be to eliminate defilements, to get rid of selfishness. The Buddha taught the wisdom that can eradicate the clinging to the idea of self, but if one does not learn to get rid of stinginess and clings to one's possessions, one cannot give up the clinging to self.

When we see that true generosity is beneficial and that selfishness and stinginess are harmful, we would like to have more moments of generosity. However, in spite of our wishes, we notice that unwholesome types of consciousness often arise. Then we are disappointed with ourselves. We should acquire understanding of what conditions the arising of unwholesome consciousness. We must have been full of attachment, aversion and ignorance in the past, even in past lives. Such tendencies have become deeply rooted; they have been accumulated. What is past has gone already, but the unwholesome tendencies that have been accumulated can condition the arising of unwholesome consciousness at the present time.

We have accumulated not only tendencies to evil but also inclinations to the wholesome. That is why there can also be moments of generosity and kindness at the present time. When an unwholesome type of consciousness arises we accumulate more unwholesomeness; when a wholesome type arises we accumulate more wholesomeness.

The Buddha taught different ways of developing wholesomeness, and when we learn about these ways there are already conditions for more wholesomeness. We find opportunity for generosity not only while we are giving but also before the actual giving, when we try to obtain the things we intend to give, and afterwards when we recollect our giving. When we are honest with ourselves we can notice that before, during and after the giving, opportunities for generosity are often spoilt by unwholesome consciousness. We may get tired when we have to buy or prepare the gift, and then aversion arises. While we are giving the gift the receiver may be ungrateful and fail to respond to our gift in the way we expected, and then we may be disappointed.

However, when we have right understanding of what wholesomeness is, we should be concerned only with developing wholesome states of mind and not with the reactions of other people. Wholesomeness is wholesomeness and nobody else can change the wholesome consciousness that arises. Before we learnt about the Buddha's teachings we did not consider generosity in this way, we did not pay attention to the moments of consciousness. Through the Buddha's teachings we learn about things as they really are. After the act of giving the opportunity to recollect our generosity with wholesome consciousness can be wasted by unwholesome consciousness. At first we may have been generous, but afterwards we may find that the gift was too expensive and regret having spent our money.

The Buddha taught that there is no self that can exert power over the different types of consciousness that arise; they arise because of their appropriate conditions. Through his teachings we can learn about the different types of consciousness and about our accumulated tendencies. Thus there will be more understanding of what is real, and this too is wholesome. When one has accumulated the tendency to stinginess it is difficult to be generous, but through the understanding of what the Buddha taught inclinations can be changed.

We read in the commentary to the Sudhābhojana Jātaka (Stories of the Buddha's Former Births, Jātakas, Book V, No. 535) about a monk in the Buddha's time who practised the utmost generosity. He gave away his food, and if he received drink sufficient to fill the hollow of his hand, he would, free from greed, still give it away. But formerly he used to be so stingy that "he would not give so much as a drop of oil on the tip of a blade of grass." In one of his past lives, when he was named Kosiya, he lived as a miser. One day he had a craving for rice porridge. When his wife suggested that she would cook porridge not only for him but also for all the inhabitants of Benares, he felt "just as if he had been struck on the head with a stick." Then his wife offered to cook for a single street, or only for the attendants in his house, only for the family, only for the two of them, but he turned down all her offers. He wanted porridge cooked for himself alone, in the forest, so that nobody else could see it. The Bodhisatta, who was at that time the god Sakka, wanted to convert him and came to him with four attendants disguised as brahmins. One by one they approached the miser and begged for some of his porridge. Sakka spoke the following stanza, praising generosity (387):

> From little one should little give, from moderate means likewise,
> From much give much: of giving nothing no question can arise.
> This then I tell you, Kosiya, give alms of that is thine:
> Eat not alone, no bliss is his that by himself shall dine,
> By charity you may ascend the noble path divine.

Kosiya reluctantly offered them some porridge. Then one of the brahmins changed into a dog. The dog made water and a drop of it fell on Kosiya's hand. Kosiya went to the river to wash and then the dog made water in Kosiya's cooking pot. When Kosiya threatened him he changed into a "blood horse" and pursued Kosiya. Then Sakka and his attendants stood in the air and Sakka preached to Kosiya out of compassion and warned him of an unhappy rebirth. Kosiya came to understand the danger of stinginess. He gave away all his possessions and became an ascetic.

We may find it difficult to part with our possessions, but when we die we cannot take them with us. Life is short: thus when we have an opportunity for generosity we should use it in order to combat selfishness. Each moment of generosity now will condition the arising of generosity in the future.

Good deeds bring about pleasant results and bad deeds bring unpleasant results. This is the law of kamma and its fruit, of cause and effect.[2] A deed (kamma) can produce result in the form of rebirth. Wholesome kamma can produce a happy rebirth and unwholesome kamma can produce an unhappy rebirth. Besides the human plane of existence, there are other planes which are happy or unhappy. Birth in the human plane or in a heavenly plane is a happy rebirth conditioned by wholesome kamma; birth in a hell plane, as a ghost or as an animal is an unhappy rebirth conditioned by unwholesome kamma. Kamma can also produce results in the form of pleasant or unpleasant sense experiences arising in the course of

---

2. See *Kamma and Its Fruit* (Wheel No. 221/224).

life. Seeing and hearing are types of consciousness that are results of kamma. We see and hear pleasant or unpleasant objects according to the kamma that produces these experiences.

Stinginess can bring about—either in this life or in a future life—the very result we fear: loss of possessions. Generosity can bring about pleasant results, such as prosperity. However, when we perform acts of generosity we should not cling to pleasant results; clinging is unwholesome. Kamma will produce its appropriate result whether we think of it or not. While we are giving we can have right understanding of kamma and its result, without clinging. We may do good deeds with the understanding of what wholesomeness is. As we have seen, understanding is a beautiful root which may or may not accompany wholesome consciousness. When understanding accompanies the wholesome consciousness, it increases the degree of wholesomeness. We cannot make understanding arise at will; it arises when there are conditions for it. Learning what the Buddha taught is a condition for greater understanding.

There are still other ways of practising generosity, even when we do not have things to give. The appreciation of other people's good deeds is also a type of generosity. When we notice that someone else is doing a good deed we can appreciate his wholesomeness, and we may express this with words of approval and praise. We may be stingy not only with regard to our possessions but also with regard to words of praise. Gradually one can learn to be generous in appreciating the wholesomeness of others.

In Thailand I had an opportunity to learn about this way of generosity, which I had not heard of before. I received a book that was printed on the occasion of the birthday of Her Majesty Queen Sirikit of Thailand. This book mentioned many of her good works, such as promoting the teaching of Buddhism, supporting temples, improving the standard of living of the people in the provinces by setting up different projects for them. When one reads this one can sincerely admire and rejoice in the good works of Her Majesty. In Thailand I also often heard the Thais saying, "*anumodana,*" which means "thanks," with the inclination of their head and clasped hands. This they do when they respect and appreciate the wholesomeness of others, usually on occasions of presenting food to the monks or giving books on the Buddhist teachings. It can become a wholesome custom to express one's appreciation on such occasions.

When we know about this way of generosity we may remember to speak about others with wholesome consciousness. In the development of wholesomeness one has to be farsighted. One should realize that whatever wholesomeness or unwholesomeness one accumulates today will produce its effects in the future, even in future lives. One can become more adept in evaluating the circumstances one is in and the friends one has. One will then be able to judge whether or not one's surroundings and friends are favourable for the development of wholesomeness. One will know what kind of speech should be avoided, what kind of speech cultivated. Often conversation tends to be about the bad qualities of others or about useless matters which are not helpful for the development of wholesomeness. Since we often become engaged in conversation with others, we should learn how to turn the conversation into an opportunity for wholesomeness.

Another way of generosity is the "sharing" of one's wholesome deeds with others. This does not mean that other people can receive the pleasant results of our good deeds. The Buddha taught that beings are "heirs" to their deeds. We each receive the results of the deeds we have done ourselves. Sharing wholesomeness with others means that our good deeds can be the condition for the arising of wholesome consciousness in others when they rejoice in our good deeds. We can share wholesomeness even with beings in other planes of existence, provided they are in planes where they can receive the benefits.

The commentary to the Without the Walls Sutta[3] narrates that King Bimbisāra offered a meal to the Buddha and omitted to dedicate his merits to other beings. Ghosts, his relatives in a former life, had hoped for this in vain, and because they were disappointed, in their despair they made a horrible screeching noise throughout the night. The Buddha explained to King Bimbisāra why the ghosts had screeched. Then King Bimbisāra made another offering and uttered the dedication, "Let this be for those relatives." The ghosts benefitted from his gifts immediately; they had wholesome states of con-

---

3. In *The Illustrator of Ultimate Meaning (Paramatthajotikā)*, Commentary to the Minor Readings (Khuddakapātha). London: Pali Text Society, 1960.

sciousness and their sufferings were allayed. Lotus-covered pools were generated for them in which they could bathe and drink, and they took on the colour of gold. Heavenly food, heavenly clothing and heavenly palaces manifested spontaneously for their use. This story illustrates that one can share one's good deeds with departed ones. If one's departed relatives are not able to receive the merit, other beings can.

It is understandable that we are sad when we lose loved ones, but if we know how to develop what is wholesome we can find great consolation. Instead of becoming filled with sadness and aversion, we should dedicate our good deeds to all those who are able to rejoice in them, then our consciousness will be wholesome. It can become our custom to share wholesomeness with others; we need not even specify to whom we wish to dedicate it.

It is a Buddhist custom when a meal or robes are offered to monks to pour water over one's hands while the monks recite words of blessing, in order to give expression to one's intention to dedicate this deed to other beings. The water symbolizes a river which fills the ocean, and even so a wholesome deed is so plentiful that it can also be shared with others.

Good deeds are usually classified as threefold: as generosity, morality, and mental development. This threefold classification should not be considered a rigid one. Morality, or abstinence from evil deeds, can also be seen as an aspect of generosity, as an act of kindness to others. When we abstain from evil deeds we give other beings the opportunity to live in peace, free from harm. If we want to develop generosity, we should not neglect mental development—the development of wholesome states of mind. We should know when consciousness is unwholesome and when wholesome in order to develop generosity and other good qualities. Knowing more about one's different types of consciousness is mental development.

The "stream-winner" is the noble person at the first stage of enlightenment. He has developed right understanding of the different mental and physical phenomena that appear at the present moment and has seen realities as they are. With the attainment of enlightenment he experiences Nibbāna, the unconditioned reality, for the first time. At the moment of enlightenment the wrong view of self is eradicated, and with it stinginess too is destroyed. Stinginess can never arise again, and he thus has perfect generosity. An ordinary person may be able to suppress stinginess temporarily, for example, at the time of giving, but stinginess is bound to arise again so long as its accumulated tendency remains. The stream-winner, through right understanding, has eradicated the tendency to stinginess and can never be overcome by it anymore.

Learning from the Buddha's teachings how to develop wholesomeness and to eradicate defilements is the greatest blessing. Therefore the teaching of the Dhamma, the Buddha's teaching, should be considered as the giving of the highest gift. In learning what the Buddha taught and in developing wholesomeness we correct our views about what is worthwhile striving for and what is not, about what is real and what is mere illusion. Before we heard about the

Buddha's teachings we may have considered the enjoyment of pleasant sense objects to be the goal of our life. After we learn the Buddha's teachings we may gradually come to see that selfish attachment gives unrest of mind and that it is harmful to ourselves and others. We may come to understand that wholesomeness is beneficial both for ourselves and for others, that it brings peace of mind.

Our outlook on what is worthwhile in life can change. We correct our views about reality when we understand what wholesome kamma is and what unwholesome kamma is, when we understand that kamma brings its appropriate result. We correct our views when we understand that not a self but different types of consciousness, wholesome or unwholesome, motivate our deeds, when we understand that these types of consciousness arise because of different conditioning factors. There are many degrees of correcting one's views. By developing understanding of realities the wrong view of self can be eradicated, and thereby perfect generosity can emerge. The effect of learning the Dhamma should be that we become less selfish and more generous, that we have more genuine concern for other people.

THE PERFECTION OF GIVING

Ācariya Dhammapāla

The perfection of giving is to be practised by benefitting beings in many ways—by relinquishing one's happiness, belongings, body, and life to others, by dispelling their fear, and by instructing them in the Dhamma. Herein, giving is threefold by way of the object to be given: the giving of material things (*āmisadāna*), the giving of fearlessness (*abhayadāna*), and the giving of the Dhamma (*dhammadāna*). Among these, the object to be given can be twofold: internal and external. The external gift is tenfold: food, drink, garments, vehicles, garlands, scents, unguents, bedding, dwellings, and lamps. These gifts, again, become manifold by analyzing each into its constituents, e.g. food into hard food, soft food, etc. The external gift can also become sixfold when analyzed by way of sense objects: visible forms, sounds, smells, tastes, tangibles, and non-sensory objects. The sense objects, such as visible forms, become manifold when analyzed into blue, etc. So too, the external gift is manifold by way of the divers valuables and belonging, such as gems, gold, silver, pearls,

---

From the Cariyāpiṭaka Aṭṭhakathā, translated by Bhikkhu Bodhi in *The Discourse on the All-Embracing Net of Views: The Brahmajāla Sutta and Its Commentaries* (BPS, 1978), pp. 289-96, pp. 322-23.

coral, etc.; fields, land, parks, etc.; slaves, cows, buffaloes, etc.

When the Great Man (the Bodhisatta) gives an external object, he gives whatever is needed to whomever stands in need of it; and knowing by himself that someone is in need of something, he gives it even unasked, much more when asked. He gives generously, not ungenerously. He gives sufficiently, not insufficiently, when there is something to be given. He does not give because he expects something in return. And when there is not enough to give sufficiently to all, he distributes evenly whatever can be shared. But he does not give things that issue in affliction for others, such as weapons, poisons, and intoxicants. Nor does he give amusements which are harmful and lead to negligence. And he does not give unsuitable food or drink to a person who is sick, even though he might ask for it, and he does not give what is suitable beyond the proper measure.

Again, when asked, he gives to householders things appropriate for householders, and to monks things appropriate for monks. He gives to his mother and father, kinsmen and relatives, friends and colleagues, children, wife, slaves, and workers, without causing pain to anyone. Having promised an excellent gift, he does not give something mean. He does not give because he desires gain, honour, or fame, or because he expects something in return, or out of expectation of some fruit other than the supreme enlightenment. He does not give detesting the gift or those who ask. He does not give a discarded object as a gift, not even to unrestrained beggers who revile and abuse him.

Invariably he gives with care, with a serene mind, full of compassion. He does not give through belief in superstitious omens: but he gives believing in kamma and its fruit.

When he gives he does not afflict those who ask by making them do homage to him, etc.; but he gives without afflicting others. He does not give a gift with the intention of deceiving others or with the intention of injuring; he gives only with an undefiled mind. He does not give a gift with harsh words or a frown, but with words of endearment, congenial speech, and a smile on his face.

Whenever greed for a particular object becomes excessive, due to its high value and beauty, its antiquity, or personal attachment, the Bodhisatta recognizes his greed, quickly dispels it, seeks out some recipients, and gives it away. And if there should be an object of limited value that can be given and a suppliant expecting it, without a second thought he bestirs himself and gives it to him, honouring him as though he were an uncelebrated sage. Asked for his own children, wife, slaves, workers, and servants, the Great Man does not give them while they are as yet unwilling to go, afflicted with grief. But when they are willing and joyful, then he gives them. But if he knows that those who ask for them are demonic beings—ogres, demons, or goblins—or men of cruel disposition, then he does not give them away. So too, he will not give his kingdom to those intent on the harm, suffering, and affliction of the world, but he would give it away to righteous men who protect the world with Dhamma.

This, firstly, is the way to practise the giving of external gifts.

The internal gift should be understood in two ways. How? Just as a man, for the sake of food and clothing, surrenders himself to another and enters into servitude and slavery, in the same way the Great Man, wishing for the supreme welfare and happiness of all beings, desiring to fulfill his own perfection of giving, with a spiritually-oriented mind, for the sake of enlightenment, surrenders himself to another and enters into servitude, placing himself at the disposal of others. Whatever limbs or organs of his might be needed by others—hands, feet, eyes, etc.—he gives them away to those who need them, without trembling and without cowering. He is no more attached to them, and no more shrinks away (from giving them to others), than if they were external objects. Thus the Great Man relinquishes an internal object in two ways: for the enjoyment of others according to their pleasure; or, while fulfilling the wishes of those who ask, for his own self-mastery. In this matter he is completely generous, and thinks: "I will attain enlightenment through non-attachment." Thus the giving of the internal gift should be understood.

Herein, giving an internal gift, he gives only what leads to the welfare of the recipient, and nothing else. The Great Man does not knowingly give his own body, limbs, and organs to Māra or to the malevolent deities in Māra's company, thinking: "Let this not lead to their harm." And likewise, he does not give to those possessed by Māra or his deities, or to madmen. But when asked for these things by others, he gives immediately, because of the rarity of such a request and the difficulty of making such a gift.

The giving of fearlessness is the giving of protection to beings when they have become frightened on account of kings, thieves, fire, water, enemies, lions, tigers, other wild beasts, dragons, ogres, demons, goblins, etc.

The giving of the Dhamma is an unperverted discourse on the Dhamma given with an undefiled mind; that is, methodical instruction conducive to good in the present life, to good in the life to come, and to ultimate deliverance. By means of such discourses, those who have not entered the Buddha's Dispensation enter it, while those who have entered it reach maturity therein.

This is the method: In brief, he gives a talk on giving, on virtue, and on heaven, on the unsatisfactoriness and defilement in sense pleasures, and on the benefit in renouncing them. In detail, to those whose minds are disposed towards the enlightenment of disciples (*sāvakabodhi*) he gives a discourse establishing and purifying them (in progress towards their goal) by elaborating upon the noble qualities of whichever among the following topics is appropriate: going for refuge, restraint by virtue, guarding the doors of the sense-faculties, moderation in eating, application to wakefulness, the seven good dhammas; application to serenity (*samatha*) by practising meditation on one of the thirty-eight objects (of serenity meditation); application to insight (*vipassanā*) by contemplating the objects of insight-interpretation such as the material body; the progressive stages of purification (*visuddhipaṭipadā*), the apprehension of the course of rightness (*sammattagahana*), the three kinds of clear knowledge (*vijjā*), the six kinds of direct knowledge (*abhiññā*), the four discriminations (*paṭisambhidā*), and the enlightenment of a disciple.

So too, for beings whose minds are disposed towards the enlightenment of paccekabuddhas and of perfectly enlightened Buddhas, he gives a discourse establishing and purifying them in the two vehicles (leading to these two types of enlightenment) by elaborating upon the greatness of the spiritual power of those Buddhas, and by explaining the specific nature, characteristic, function, etc. of the ten *pāramīs* in their three stages. Thus the Great Man gives the gift of the Dhamma to beings.

When he gives a material gift, the Great Man gives food thinking: "May I, by this gift, enable beings to achieve long life, beauty, happiness, strength, intelligence, and the supreme fruit of unsullied bliss." He gives drink wishing to allay the thirst of sensual defilements; garments to gain the adornments of shame and moral dread and the golden complexion (of a Buddha); vehicles for attaining the modes of psychic potency and the bliss of Nibbāna; scents for producing the sweet scent of virtue; garlands and unguents for producing the beauty of the Buddha-qualities; seats for producing the seat on the terrace of enlightenment; bedding for producing the bed of a Tathāgata's rest; dwellings so he might become a refuge for beings; lamps so he might obtain the five eyes.[1]

1. The five eyes are the fleshly eye (*maṁsacakkhu*); the divine eye (*dibbacakkhu*), by which he sees beings

He gives visible forms for producing the fathom-wide aura (surrounding a Buddha); sounds for producing the Brahmā-like voice (of a Buddha); tastes for endearing himself to all the world; and tangibles for acquiring a Buddha's elegance.

He gives medicines so he might later give the ageless and deathless state of Nibbāna. He gives slaves the gift of freedom so he might later emancipate beings from the slavery of the defilements. He gives blameless amusements and enjoyments in order to produce delight in the true Dhamma. He gives his own children as a gift in order that he might adopt all beings as his children by granting them an ariyan birth. He gives his wives as a gift in order that he might become master over the entire world. He gives gifts of gold, gems, pearls, coral, etc. in order to achieve the major marks of physical beauty (characteristic of a Buddha's body), and gifts of the diverse means of beautification in order to achieve the minor features of physical beauty.[2] He gives his treasuries as a gift in order to obtain the treasury of the true Dhamma; the gift of his kingdom in order to become the king of the Dhamma; the gift of monasteries, parks, ponds, and groves in order to achieve the

---

pass away and re-arise in accordance with their kamma; the wisdom eye (*paññācakkhu*), by which he sees the specific and general characteristics of things; the Buddha-eye (*buddhacakkhu*), by which he sees the propensities and dispositions of beings; and the universal eye (*samantacakkhu*), his knowledge of omniscience.

2. The thirty-two major and eighty minor characteristics of a Great Man's body.

jhānas, etc.; the gift of his feet in order that he might be marked with the auspicious wheels; the gift of his hands in order that he might give to beings the rescuing hand of the true Dhamma to help them across the four floods[3]; the gift of his ears, nose, etc. in order to obtain the spiritual faculties of faith, etc.; the gift of his eyes in order to obtain the universal eye; the gift of his flesh and blood with the thought: "May my body be the means of life for all the world! May it bring welfare and happiness to all beings at all times, even on occasions of merely seeing, hearing, recollecting, or ministering to me!" And he gives the gift of his head in order to become supreme in all the world.

Giving thus, the Great Man does not give unwillingly, nor by afflicting others, nor out of fear, moral shame, or the scolding of those in need of gifts. When there is something excellent, he does not give what is mean. He does not give extolling himself and disparaging others. He does not give out of desire for the fruit, nor with loathing for those who ask, nor with lack of consideration. Rather, he gives thoroughly, with his own hand, at the proper time, considerately, without discrimination, filled with joy throughout the three times.[4] Having given, he does not become remorseful afterwards. He does not become either conceited or obsequious in relation to the recipients, but behaves amiably towards them. Bountiful and liberal, he gives things together with a

---

3. The four floods of sensual desire, desire for existence, wrong views, and ignorance.

4. The "three times" are before presenting the gift, while giving it, and after giving it.

bonus *(saparivāra)*. For when he gives food, thinking: "I will give this along with a bonus," he gives garments, etc. as well. And when he gives garments, thinking: "I will give this along with a bonus," he gives food, etc. as well. The same method with gifts of vehicles, etc. And when he gives a gift of one of the sense objects, such as visible forms, he gives the other sense objects also as a bonus.

The gift of visible forms should be understood thus. Having gained something, such as a flower, garment, or relic of a blue, yellow, red, or white colour, etc., considering it in terms of its visible form, thinking to make a gift of a visible form, he offers it to a worthy recipient together with its base.

The gift of sounds should be understood by way of the sounds of drums, etc. It is certainly not possible to give a sound as one gives a cluster of lotuses, tearing it out by its bulb and roots and placing it in the hands. But one gives a gift of sound by giving its base. Thus he makes a gift of sound by presenting a musical instrument, such as drums or tom toms, to the Triple Gem; or by giving medicine for the voice, such as oil and molasses, to preachers of the Dhamma; or by announcing a lecture on the Dhamma, chanting the scriptures, giving a discourse on the Dhamma, holding a discussion, or expressing appreciation for the good deeds of others.

The gift of scents is made when, after getting a delightfully scented object, such as scented roots, powdered scent, etc., considering it in terms of its scent, thinking to make a gift of scent, he offers it to the Triple Gem. He relinquishes a scented object such as agaru or sandalwood, for the purpose of making an offering of scent.

The gift of tastes is made when, after getting a delightfully flavoured object, such as flavoured roots, etc., considering it in terms of its taste, thinking to make a gift of taste, he gives it to worthy recipients. Or he relinquishes a flavourful object, such as grain, cows, etc.[5]

The gift of tangibles should be understood by way of beds, chairs, etc. and by way of coverlets and mantels, etc. For having gained some soft, delightful, blameless tangible object, such as a bed, chair, cushion, pillow, undergarment, or uppergarment, considering it in terms of its tangible qualities, thinking to make a gift of a tangible item, he gives it to worthy recipients; having gained the aforesaid tangible objects, he relinquishes them.

The gift of mental objects (*dhammadāna*) should be understood by way of nutriment, drink, and life, since it is the mental-object base which is here intended.[6] Having gained a delightful object such as nutriment, considering it as part of the mental-object base, thinking to make a gift of a non-sensory object, he gives nutriment—i.e. ghee, butter, etc., or a drink—i.e. the eight kinds of drink such as mango juice, etc.;

---

5. Doubtlessly the commentator means cows as a source for the "five delicacies"—milk, curd, butter, ghee, and cream of ghee—not as a source of beefsteak.

6. *Dhamma* here, as the context indicates, means the sixth type of object, not the Buddha's teaching. This class of object includes the nutritive essence of food and the life faculty, hence the explanation that follows in the text.

or, considering it a gift of life, he gives a ticket-meal or a fortnightly meal, etc., gets doctors to wait upon the sick and afflicted, liberates animals from a net, has a fishing net or bird-cage destroyed, releases prisoners from prison, causes an injunction to be given forbidding the slaughter of animals, or undertakes any action of a similar nature for the sake of protecting the life of beings.

This entire accomplishment in giving he dedicates to the welfare and happiness of the whole world, and to his own unshakable emancipation through supreme enlightenment. He dedicates it to the attainment of inexhaustible desire (for the good), inexhaustible concentration, ingenuity, knowledge, and emancipation. In practising the perfection of giving the Great Being should apply the perception of impermanence to life and possessions. He should consider them as shared in common with many, and should constantly and continuously arouse great compassion towards beings. Just as, when a house is blazing, the owner removes all his property of essential value and himself as well without leaving anything important behind, so does the Great Man invariably give, without discrimination and without concern.

When the Great Man has made a mental determination to completely relinquish whatever possessions come his way, whether animate or inanimate, there are four shackles to giving (which he must overcome), namely, not being accustomed to giving in the past, the inferiority of the object to be given, the excellence and beauty of the object, and worry over the loss of the object.

(1) When the Bodhisatta possesses objects that can be given and suppliants are present, but his mind does not leap up at the thought of giving and he does not want to give, he should conclude: "Surely, I have not been accustomed to giving in the past, therefore a desire to give does not arise now in my mind. So that my mind will delight in giving in the future, I will give a gift. With an eye for the future let me now relinquish what I have to those in need." Thus he gives a gift—generous, openhanded, delighting in relinquishing, one who gives when asked, delighting in giving and in sharing. In this way the Great Being destroys, shatters, and eradicates the first shackle to giving.

(2) Again, when the object to be given is inferior or defective, the Great Being reflects: "Because I was not inclined to giving in the past, at present my requisites are defective. Therefore, though it pains me, let me give whatever I have as a gift even if the object is low and inferior. In that way I will, in the future, reach the peak in the perfection of giving." Thus he gives whatever kind of gift he can—generous, openhanded, delighting in relinquishing, one who gives when asked, delighting in giving and in sharing. In this way the Great Being destroys, shatters, and eradicates the second shackle to giving.

(3) When a reluctance to give arises due to the excellence or beauty of the object to be given, the Great Being admonishes himself: "Good man, haven't you made the aspiration for the supreme enlightenment, the loftiest and most superior of all states? Well then, for the sake of enlightenment, it is proper

for you to give excellent and beautiful objects as gifts." Thus he gives what is excellent and beautiful —generous, open-handed, delighting in relinquishing, one who gives when asked, delighting in giving and in sharing. In this way the Great Man destroys, shatters, and eradicates the third shackle to giving.

(4) When the Great Being is giving a gift, and he sees the loss of the object being given, he reflects thus: "This is the nature of material possessions, that they are subject to loss and to passing away. Moreover, it is because I did not give such gifts in the past that my possessions are now depleted. Let me then give whatever I have as a gift, whether it be limited or abundant. In that way I will, in the future, reach the peak in the perfection of giving." Thus he gives whatever he has as a gift—generous, open-handed, delighting in relinquishing, one who gives when asked, delighting in giving and in sharing. In this way the Great Being destroys, shatters, and eradicates the fourth shackle to giving.

Reflecting upon them thus in whatever way is appropriate is the means for dispelling the harmful shackles to the perfection of giving. The same method used for the perfection of giving also applies to the perfection of virtue and the other perfections.

ABOUT THE CONTRIBUTORS

BHIKKHU BODHI is a Buddhist monk of American nationality, originally from New York City. Ordained in Sri Lanka in 1972, he has been Editor for the BPS since 1984 and its President since 1988.

LILY DE SILVA is Professor of Pali and Buddhist Studies at the University of Peradeniya in Sri Lanka. A regular contributor to Buddhist scholarly and popular journals, she is also the editor of the subcommentary to the Dīgha Nikāya, published by the Pali Text Society of London.

SUSAN ELBAUM JOOTLA is an American Buddhist living in northern India and a long-term practitioner of vipassana meditation in the tradition of Sayagyi U Ba Khin. Her previous BPS publications include *Investigation for Insight* (Wheel No. 301/302) and *Inspiration from Enlightened Nuns* (Wheel No. 349/350).

NINA VAN GORKOM is a Dutch Buddhist who first encountered Buddhism in Thailand. A keen student of the Abhidhamma, she is the author of *Buddhism in Daily Life* and *Abhidhamma in Daily Life.*

M.O'C. WALSHE has been an active Buddhist since 1951 and is a past chairman of the English Sangha Trust. He is the author of numerous articles on Buddhism and translator of the complete Dīgha Nikāya under the title *Thus Have I Heard: The Long Discourses of the Buddha* (London: Wisdom, 1987).

Of related interest from The Wheel Series

THE BUDDHIST LAYMAN

Selected essays on living the Buddhist life as a layperson. R. Bogoda: Principles of Lay Buddhism; Susan Jootla: Right Livelihood; M.O'C. Walshe: Having Taken the First Step; Detachment.

Wheel No. 294/295 — 75 pages

ONE FOOT IN THE WORLD

Lily de Silva

In this small book, subtitled "Buddhist Approaches to Present-day Problems," Dr. de Silva discusses such vital issues as dealing with stress, Buddhist attitudes to gain and honour, livelihood and development, facing death without fear, the human body, and Buddhism and modern sensualism.

Wheel No. 337/338 — 64 pages

GEMSTONES OF THE GOOD DHAMMA

Ven. S. Dhammika

This small anthology brings together verses from the Pali scriptures, arranged by subject with Pali and English on facing pages. Chapters deal with giving, virtue, speech, wealth, friendship, love, etc.

Wheel No. 342/344 — 81 pages

Prices as in latest catalog

For release by May 1990

THE UDĀNA

Inspired Utterances of the Buddha

Translated from the Pali by
John D. Ireland

The *Udāna* is one of the loveliest and most uplifting texts in the Pali Canon, a collection of eighty short but deeply impressive suttas. Opening at the foot of the Bodhi tree shortly after the Buddha's enlightenment, the *Udāna* records some of the best known incidents in the Master's life: his paeon of victory over the forces of darkness; his instruction to Bāhiya on "sudden awakening"; the story of Nanda and the celestial nymphs; the parable of the blind men and the elephant; the solemn Nibbāna suttas; and much more. Like the *Dhammapada*, the *Udāna* will be a constant friend and adviser for frequent reading and reflection. It will also make a much appreciated gift to offer to friends receptive to the Dhamma. This new translation combines precision with clarity and also includes over 25 pages of notes drawn mostly from the Udāna Commentary.

160 pages
Softback

Please inquire about price
ISBN 955-24-0055-4

THE BUDDHIST PUBLICATION SOCIETY

is an approved charity dedicated to making known the Teaching of the Buddha, which has a vital message for people of all creeds.

Founded in 1958, the BPS has published a wide variety of books and booklets covering a great range of topics. Its publications include accurate annotated translations of the Buddha's discourses, standard reference works, as well as original contemporary expositions of Buddhist thought and practice. These works present Buddhism as it truly is—a dynamic force which has influenced receptive minds for the past 2500 years and is still as relevant today as it was when it first arose.

A full list of our publications will be sent free of charge upon request. Write to:

The Hony. Secretary
BUDDHIST PUBLICATION SOCIETY
P.O. Box 61
54, Sangharaja Mawatha
Kandy Sri Lanka